To Brian, With many thanks for your
support in Writers' Group over the
years and heres to our shared love
of the natural world.
        With best wishes, David.
                8/3/24.

TORRIDGE
River Gallery

DAVID CURTIS

Illustrations by

Cressida Lowery

THE CHOIR PRESS

First published in the United Kingdom in 2024 by
The Choir Press

ISBN 978-1-78963-434-1

Dedication

Inspired by the North Devon countryside, the Curtis family and Writers' Cramp.

David Curtis was born in Bideford and grew up in Beaford, twelve miles inland. He taught English in comprehensive schools in Swindon, Blandford Forum and Thatcham and in a folkehogskole in Norway and he advised on teaching and the curriculum in the West Midlands. David and his wife live in Solihull. Their two children, William and Hannah and their families, live nearby.

Cressida is a Devon based designer and has created lino cut prints to illustrate the poems in her distinctive, characterful style. Gaining a degree in textile design at Camberwell School of Art, Cressida's love of pattern and surface texture continues to enrich her work. She works mainly in two mediums, lino for printmaking and precious metals for jewellery design. Freelancing for the luxury end of the market, her work has exhibited at notable galleries and stores worldwide and at outlets locally. She draws inspiration from Devon's flora, fauna, architecture and landmarks.

With special thanks to Writers' Cramp members: Graham Affleck, Glena Baptiste, Dallin Chapman, Brian Chase, Heather Harrison, Martin Hayes, Theresa Jones and Pamela Vaughan, and the poet and critical friend, David Donaldson.

And to Cressida Lowery for her very beautiful linocut work.

Contents

River Gallery

Growing Pains

It was safe there,
an always warm
home, a pink arm
protecting him,
a soft cubbyhole,
almost a womb;

then slowly less room
in which to snuggle:
he was pushed,
daily,
remorselessly
off his once ample lap.

And she left him,
for three long days,
returning not alone
but with a bawling,
clutching, smelly
stranger in his place.

He left, was lost
till father found him
curled nose to knee
in a dark, old
tea chest
in their garden.

He wouldn't come out
for father. Mother
coaxed him out,
drew him to her,
dried his face,
cuddled him.

Still at times
he would sit warm
on his mother's lap
loved and safe,
but, besides,
now he was grown.

Jackdaw Quarry

There was no air there
in her parlour where the black piano stood,
just dust and choking musk.

He steadied the stool,
flexed stiff fingers, flinched from the spilt lexicon
of jumbling hieroglyphs:

Beethoven's Sonata in G,
bold across the page top, and under, a blur
of gashes and swollen stops.

He steered his middle finger
tentatively towards F sharp and G sharp
jarred like a bad tooth:

a note, a pause, another note,
a false note, a longer pause, no melody
nor any rhythm.

Miss Darch, faded
as the half-drawn curtains, shuffled, wheezed,
evinced a strangled cough.

He'd scaled the Quarry's shale,
bike tipped in the grass, piano lesson still
an hour and two miles away.

Deep inside the rock hole
shone a jackdaw's slate-grey eyes,
feathers warming her eggs.

In her domain she nestled,
settled on her oak twig throne, indifferent
to this sudden upstart boy

who, for a brief eternity,
entered her world of oxygen and stone.
He absorbs her hoard

of beer can rings, yellow rag,
silver paper, five p pieces, her primeval stench
piercing his virgin nose.

He hangs there, birdlike,
blasted by Atlantic winds, clinging to rock,
feet bedded on grit.

He might have practised,
put aside half hour a day to tackle scales,
play sonatas, pass grades;

instead he'd climbed high
to a mother jackdaw's lair, to her ripe wildness,
her voluptuous smell.

Piano will feature one day
in his life; but now it's feral jackdaw-witchery
hammers his blood.

The Draw of Sunbeams

It starts on Clovelly Heights
spluttering to life like a birth-choked babe
I watch it struggling to stay in air

while grasses smother it
drizzles mist its breath
mud clogs its gurglings

inquisitive visitors come to stare
in green, laced wellies
with visions and theodolites

it gains strength in fits and starts
bodily broadens deepens
gathers pace and purpose

gulls drift white heralds overhead
rushes part on either side
marsh marigolds tossed crowns

its a journey beginning in brown
brightening to brick yellow
seams of red and back to brown

beds of granite and soft clays
dipper dapper on a rock
kingfisher kaleidescopic

a boistrous sister falls off the moors
they come together naturally
laugh and shine

a wodwo watches the flow wades in
writes the mystery
the awe of water running

a storyteller walking the bank feels
the pull of tides sees bellies gleam
plots an otter's story

under many stone and iron arches
passes weakened by thrown leavings
till sea salt smarts heals

there is a draw of sunbeams
clouds flocking Dartmoor sheep
darken and there's rain

it starts on Clovelly Heights
spluttering to life like a birth-choked babe
I watch it struggling to stay in air

An Old Stink

Behind me the shed, its clinging stink
of half- cured, worn-bare moleskins,
stretched and nailed to dry on an old door,
lop-sided rectangles, six inches by four;

of my two ferrets, their animal smell
rising from musty straw like acid bile,
in clammy vapours -try skinning their kin
the weasel - a reek to bare your brain;

of my table-museum rich in animal remains:
the grubbed up skulls of fox and rabbit, rain-
bleached rams' horns, owl pellets, immured-
in-mouse-fur fragments of bone: bone-hoard;

as though there was a drainage underground
to this shed from the village graveyard;
from that part of Beaford Moor to which wild
wolves in packs were shepherded and killed;

the stench has seeped its way down roots
so indelibly that chemicals can't shift it;
it nourishes my body like a blood stream,
will not be exorcised by art or time.

Honey

The beech tree stood tall
bark smooth as young skin,
protected by moss
a deep fissure,
bees flying in,
swollen leg sacks
golden with pollen,
and out to gather more.

We light a sulphur candle,
hold and press it
tight against the crack,
intent on causing
sleepiness or worse,
hoping to penetrate
past the doped bees
to their honey store.

We couldn't force
our fingers down
inside this slit
to the wild bees'
sticky trove,
withdraw comb,
honey dripping,
to sate our craving.

In our wake, carnage,
dead bees littering
their secret place,
bark blacked by smoke,
smeech of smouldering
wood and carcasses
polluting clean air.
Homeward, heads drooped.

Two Buzzards, Circling

It rolls, but safe in my hand's palm,
ovoid, creamy white,
and blotched with flecks of reds and browns,
liver spots, clustered at the more blunt end,
matching the mottled colours
of the parents' feathers.

I cradle it. It's delicate, the shell thin
from age and nibbling mites
who've colonised its bed of sawdust.
I stole it from a nest on Beaford Moor,
me in my early teens, found the nest,
climbed the tree, took the egg,

pierced each end with a bramble thorn
and blew the embryonic infant out,
keeping this violated shell. If, all those years ago,
that foetus had been left to grow, those cells
had multiplied to form hooked beak, needle eyes,
the features of a magisterial bird,

buzzard, feathered, taloned, ready to pitch
into accommodating air, to fly.
I remember the oak, the tree's fork,
the easy climb, attendant lapwings
flashing blacks and whites, meadow pipit pairs,
melting the sky a curlew's cry.

I can picture in this eggshell's globe
that callow, country boy,
his knees mud-caked and scratched.
He could lead you even now over the moor
to rare white heather, to a remote pine copse
canopied with raven's nests.

Above parkland in this West Midlands town
I watch two buzzards driven northwards,
riding thermals, spread finger-feathers
nursing weather, silently scribing circles
above noise, seeking a safe tree.
I feel an updraft lift me from the ground.

Artful Fox

This small planet has hosted evenings by the million,
thousands lived through by homo sapiens
and Tuesday's started same as usual-
big round Summer sun sinking behind the birch tree,
clouds in gold and bluish strips bright as a Hockney,
me, preoccupied, on the patio, a Guinness
and a barely troubled crossword on the paving.

At first I didn't see the fox. Then he was there
standing stock still on the lawn.
He had two routes, one past the fir trees
and through the broken fence into the neighbours';
the other, skirting the lawn to the back door,
and back, out through the same gap.
I rarely saw him, but I fed him, stowing
left-over meat behind the greenhouse.
Always gone by morning.

This evening he'd come early on his way and stopped.
And stared. At me. Tall fox, thin, pale brown,
he stood like a messenger sent
from his home of trees and running water,
to remind me that too much focus on
bank accounts and mobile phones, headlines
and deadlines were sapping my spirit.

Fox stood there. 'Look at me', he seemed to say. 'Look!
Aren't I a handsome specimen of foxhood? Stop! Look!
Look at the flowers on the shrub that frames me.
Look at the forming apples, the new green on the birch tree
soaring above me. At who shares your table, shares your bed.
Next time you fetch the newspaper
or turn a diary page, remember Fox!'
He trotted through the fence, leaving a tremble
in the air against the flowering hydrangia.

Sacrifice

Peaking to tip the heavens
foam crests hair,
salt crusts sweat
silvering forehead and arm,
race against wave, and time,
wrists within grasp, if one soul
only were saved,
and will be,
though horizon curves away
and where stars were no light.

Pebbles gleam and grey, gleam and grime,
slide, grind grit to shingle, sand to slime.

Trough. Gut bloats throat,
flesh leaves bone, boat
lead weight drops
to rusty hulk, a claw,
angled jawbones,
bladderwort wreathes,
below light
to bottom
to sudden undertow,
to the gutteral sighs of the sea.

Pebbles are dragged and tossed, dragged and thrown,
day and night, breakers batter rocks, wear granite down.

Toast. Tea. Sister Florence's
marmalade-tang,
stepping on grass,
cat-purr, fence-chat,
to look forward,
joy in words, touch;
a life
lost
to stone, bone, shell, sand,
to tide: leaves a cold bed, an empty hand.

On a pebble in a rock pool, water placid and warm,
sits a lifeboatman's daughter, protected from harm.

Lords of Misrule

hush hush Old Grey feels the light thin
leaves his treehole feathers air
moon throws shadow arrow over fields
he hangs beak hook
eyes blades keen for grass twitch
Owl's each rash shrew his

into his meadow from dark tunnelled holt
Badger enters face black white black
fear the angled devil's mask
skull so thick an axe won't split it
jaw once set can't unclench it
only enemy vain man

fright of Bat skin-winged bone
ghoulish leather-eared rat-head
clogs blackest nightmares
between trees clots air
swooping snags hair tis said
tooths neck sucks blood

over kitchen floors Cockroaches
black knights hydra-hardy
squash one three take its place
out of cobwebbed caves scuttle
tar armour gleaming
masticate defecate mate

rise as man's garish daystar sinks
commandeer the night.

Dartmoor Gothic

Outside, kneebone, hipbone, breast and shoulder
rise from the peat in tablelands and tors.
The Old Mother dozes, and in a fold,
a farmhouse lies, thatch roofed, slate floored.

A woman is one by one, Lover, Mother, Layer-out.
She turns the world. With her adaptive hands
she blesses infants, pleases partners, washes
the bodies of those whose souls have fled.

Inside, the supper done, the ham and tongue,
pickles and cheese devoured, the party huddles
round an open fire, and over beverages tales are told
hinting that even thick cob walls are permeable.

In the darkest hour of every night the peace
of our hosts' matrimonial bed is broken
from below, by racketting like dry leaves
battering against a sheet of corrogated iron.

It fell to the man to leave the bed's warm draw,
and, dressing gown pulled round him for the chill,
descend the tunnelling stair, and, Orpheus-like,
bring the riddle's answer up to the waiting world.

Dartmoor was closer to nature then: electricity
had yet to power these homes; floors were slate
or mother rock, some softened by a sheepskin rug.
Lumination was by tilly lamp or naked candle flame.

He lit a night light, toed the cold floor, dropped
step by step towards the pandemonium,
the flame flickering as he fought the dark,
towards an oak door shutting off the apple room.

Was it a frantic animal clawing to break free,
or bats' wings beating out a dead march?
He stood there in encroaching dark, sweating
despite the cold; and squeezed the metal apse.

A fist of icy wind numbed him, beat him back,
gutted his candle, doused the ashes in the hearth.
The entrance to the apple store's black vault
seemed like a threshold, screening life from death.

In bed again he fought to warm his frozen blood,
clung to body-heat. What had been a bright home,
full of song and mischief, became uneasy,
gloomy as a stagnant well, quieter than a tomb.

Wild ponies lift from their grazing as the guests,
oppressed by the weight of hanging questions,
seek their ways home through twisting lanes,
under granite megaliths and standing stones.

What the Owl Says

I can't see the face of the owl in the before-dawn
black, only hear her hooked question,
feel a gnawing, hour-of-the-wolf pain.

On the Parsonage wall a nesting greenfinch sang;
until my casually aimed bullet killed her song

and left a gap on the red brick wall, a hole
that no amount of busyness has filled;

in my young hand, clammy with adrenalin,
a rabbit's heart, drained of blood, still thumping,

in the trodden grass, the carcass, nose still wet,
its moist guts ripped out through a belly cut;

old Janny Rogers smiled in Bid-e-more Lane,
as my arcing shotgun snapped a pigeon's wing.

Careless, then, to the singularity of a gambolling
hare, a home-bound swallow, rowan leaves uncurling.

The clock chimes four and I lie in my bed alone
with memories, like the feather, fur and bone
in an owl's pellet, reminding me of undigested pain.

To See a Kingfisher

To see a kingfisher, walk down Mill Lane
to the river. At Beaford Bridge
go through the last gate on the right,
an iron gate on granite posts,
and cross the flood plain.

You'll face the gamekeeper!
He'll drive his mini-tractor up to you
as you reach the river bank,
ask if you've a permit to fish,
you with only a birch switch in your hand.
He'll complain that his pheasant pullets will fly
across the water if disturbed, be shot
by strangers, losing his boss fun and money.
Sitting astride his loud machine—
dogs angled out barking– he'll order
you away: you're trespassing.

Retrace your steps, cross the bridge,
go right again and walk a mile under
Yeory fir plantation, round the leftward sweep
of the Torridge under Pink Hill Farm—
pink for the Royalist Blood of 1646—
to three alder trees,
buzzard feathers often underfoot,
and a dead and barkless oak.
Here, you might raise a heron,
cranking into air, all too long bones,
arthritic off the shingle.
Here, the river straightens,
the water flow slow, quiet.

Now! Yes!
Gone!
a wild child's crayon,
a trail of orange/blue
slashed across blank sky,
a dart, a spirit,
irridescent,
splitting air,
divides before and after.

In times to come, you can tell your grandchildren—
'One day, under Pink Hill, I saw a kingfisher'.

Building a Wall

He picked a heavy stone up from a pile of stones
beside a fir tree, under a crab apple branch,
turned it over in his hand:
twenty seven woodlice sheltering;

the last stone in a row of stones
for a low wall between path and patch
of garden dug and flattened for wild flowers,
a cherry and a plum tree.

What if one of these woodlice should die,
crushed between his shuffling stones?
Does a woodlouse' life have worth? Or an apple's,
hanging from the weighed down branch?

A neighbour leans over the fence, whispers:
her husband who had just shopped in the town,
returning, feeling queasy,
retired to bed, has died.

He dug a hole for the stone, rammed it firm,
first dusting off the woodlice with his hand
so that they fell to soft ground
near their home in stones.

Woodlice appear like warty blotches,
indistinguishable one from one, yet
each one has a corrugated beauty
and a dedicated will to live.

At sunset the apples briefly glow, the stones cast
shadows on the earth. He watches as his neighbour's
kitchen light goes off, pictures her
climbing the steep staircase to their bed.

The Three Chicks have Fledged

She came down the path as twilight thickened,
knowing her way, stick in hand.
We offered a seat on the bench but she
was a walker, she said. We told her we'd come
for a view of the osprey's nest, over the lake.

It was hard in the evening to make out the nest,
not in the obvious trees by the shore,
but further into the island in shrub.
Her eyes were so clear, her knowledge so real,
her experience so lengthy and learnt from,

she was able to pinpoint through tree-line
and finely judged distance the spot
where dark clustered close to the ground.
'The three chicks have fledged', she said
after some minutes' reflection.

'The female leaves first. The male stays on,
teaching the nestlings to fish, then he leaves.
He's returned every year for ten years or more'.
We talked with this woman for less than an hour.
While she smiled her farewell, her eyes

never left for a moment the nest,
this woman of ninety, whose offspring
were ospreys. She'd lived with their ways,
grown with them as they grew,
flown with them when they flew.

The Street

Her bees were busy all season,
buzzing, heathers to ceanothus,
filling their legbags
and back to their hives.

With her hot knife she trimmed
the wax caps, letting honey
run from their combs
as her extractor spun.

Into her sterilized honeypots
sticky amber liquid streamed
to each jar's brim; the jars
screwed tight and labelled.

He rose early, drove to the shop
and the fruit and veg shelves,
snatched two Seville cartons,
set them on the kitchen table

by his short-bladed knife,
bowl for pith, bowl for skins,
string, muslin bag,
thermometer, clock, huge pan,

and got to work: scraped, sliced,
strained, boiled hard, tested,
matched tops to jars,
filled each with marmalade.

Two weeks' later, in the street,
each gave the other gold;
in the quiet of their homes
they spread their gifts and fed.

Chainsaw 1

There's a space outside my window where the tree stood.
They say a tree grows for a third of life, lives
in its pomp a third, and for the last third dies.

I watched my tree yield over time to time: fat mulberries,
then smaller, fewer fruit, then not a single fruit;
palm sized to fewer, smaller leaves.

In its pomp my tree would splatter unsuspecting passers-by
with deep scarlet juice, leave the pavement
pocked with blood-red bombs.

While other trees leafed in early Spring, my mulberry
lingered, didn't send out leaves till April time,
green flags to greet arriving swifts.

It was cut down, savaged by a chainsaw's teeth, after
a self-styled 'surgeon', seeking work, had warned
that a falling tree could cause an accident.

At first he sawed some inner branches out: it looked
like careful pruning. Then the other branches.
Finally, he sliced up the trunk.

It had been my intention when my mulberry fell, to save
the trunk and lay it in my wild flower patch
for birds and animals to nest and forage in,

but once the chainsaw's rasp had raped the street's
tranquility, and the leading branch was lopped,
I couldn't face the desolation.

I have no doubt the wound outside my house will heal.
Perhaps one day I'll plant another mulberry
or next door's holly will fill its place.

There was a ribbed, round scar at head height on the trunk,
where a branch thought dangerous had grown.
Woodworms had holed the soft wood centre.

Deep fissures etched its bark. Each year a branch or two
dried out, turned grey and died. I'd like my mulberry
to have met its end with grace and quietly.

30

Chainsaw 2

Father, why are you so distressed
when you couldn't have done more than your best?
Trees, just like you and me grow,
mature, wither, then die, we know,
and, though our much treasured beech
was not given a fair chance to reach
its full glory, despite all you did to persuade
them to respect the home we had made,
those mercenaries conducted a raid
arriving before sunrise with chainsaws,
haloed in black by panicking crows and jackdaws,
woke us from our youthful, innocent sleep.
What they have sowed, so may they reap.
An irreplaceable beech tree has been felled,
a friend of the family wilfully killed.

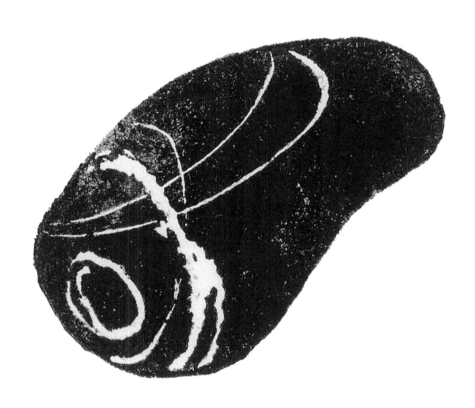

Lucky Stone

Take this lucky stone, shaped
like a knucklebone, a carpal
or an inner-ear bone, anvil;
size of a hare's kidney and
colour, blood red brown;

smooth, too, one side
concave so a thumb can buff it
in a pocket, grooved
to a snug hollow.
It's gravid, like the core

of something, an ancient pip,
a kernel very old and waiting
for an age before it might
send down a shoot to wet ground,
another up into light to grow

a flower yellow as the sun.
You gave it me. It bears
the weight of years. Stow it
in your purse and sometimes
take it in your hand. Its shape

remains the same although I've
nursed it daily in the crook of
thumb, fore and middle finger
warmed its cold consistency:
monkey nut, kidney bean, tiny

folded embryo. Treasure it, this
token. I'll leave it at your door
among your trampled sea
shells. Don't lose it. A stone
merely. But feel its heaviness.

And we saw a woodcock

The first stile is easy, and
I'm on my way.
There's thyme in the air
and a scrape of salt
from the ocean over the hill.
I fill my lungs,
swish through grass, bend
to the tug of a slope
and thrill to the pull
of muscles tight on the hem
of my shorts. I'm
young again, young with
the power to climb
without pant or pause.

At the summit I stop to scan
valley, forest and fields,
oak trees expansive
where hedges once held
the land to garden sized plots;
now blue and green stripes
of linseed and rape, wheat
beige in twenty five acre lots;
the sea to the west,
gathering, gathering:
a wave crests, curls white,
folds on itself, breaks,
peters through shingle.

Down a ditch arcs a woodcock,
sharp headed arrow,
swift, direct,
a witchbird riding wind,
a shy bird of the wild,
Plato's bird bird, beak
curved bone
from beyond.
And gone.
The way-sign points inland,
I stride down a lane

at three miles an hour,
breeze at my back,
a bounce in my step,
heart a kite.
Instead of lifting the apse
I vault a gate.
I've lived woodcock.

Clouds bunch, breeze falls.
Backpack straps
pinch; blisters
on my heel nip;
old knee bones nag.
The air is heavy.
Drizzle mists glasses.
I pull on waterproofs,
wait to turn home.

Earth puddles to mud,
sticks to the soles
and sides of my boots;
my step push slips.
I bribe myself on:
at the towpath a drink.
My backpack I shift
off its sweat patch,
take short steps, talk less.
Breathing is shallow;
blisters weep; knee
tendons clench and ache.
One more stile before home.

I bend, unlace my boots
at the pub door,
enjoy just to sit,
sip beer slowly,
eat a hearty beef stew.
We did all right,
kept a good pace.
Shared thoughts
on family, health, work,
government. Got on well.
And we saw a woodcock.

The Village Pump

It wears granite, white-powders bones,
sifts them, drifts them till they merge with earth,
feeds the lime tree avenue from graveyard gate to church door,
flycatchers flitting twig to twig, rooks in the chestnuts,
wets and grouts the cobbles down Church Street
hopscotch of dandelions and wood sorrell, seeping
under the main road and, over the road, the Globe inn.

At sunrise, aproned women gather from low doors
with jugs to carry water from the pump's lead mouth,
startling the sleeping folk to waking with their racket.
They laugh: Sarah, fat fingers at the handle,
Rotha, fateful, fox-blood fretting her old cheeks,
pig-blood redding her nails, and sharp-elbowed Margaret,
chapped lips humming 'How Great Thou Art', standing by.

The village floats on water. Wells riddle Towell Meadow,
Cooksworthy Lane, house after house, and here, at the hub
between Shop Corner, Pub and Graveyard, the main-spring
flushing out spiders and mole in his water-tight coat.
Beneath the cobbles, through yellow clay, waters seep,
a trickle below hearing, beneath the scratch
of Sarah's tale-telling and Rotha's Delphic grate.

Sieving through soil, it undresses bones,
caresses them to dust, levening red Devon earth.
The women harvest water, gossip, bear it to kitchens.
Insistent as oak tree buds, rivulets of water teem,
damping roots, shifting cargoes place to place,
unseen unless the aproned women pump the water out,
or after heavy downpour, blocked drains flood the street.

Domain: 2022

There are no politics in Lydford Wood,
no women cowering from tyrants' guns,
no lies, no screaming syrens,
no overbearing sense of self
in his wood of ancient oaks, holly for remembrance,
alder out of damp earth, beech saplings,
splashes of marsh marigold over lush grass,
and the brook following its slow, chosen path.

The old fella, safe under a fern-clad,
hay-lined cave of hazel branches,
tugs his beard, tunes to the buzzard
mewing from a queenly oaktree's fork,
hears the brook's murmur, running
through clay, rattling on stone; familiar songs,
and sights, an acrobatic, dapper nuthatch,
a flurry of long tailed tits exploring gorse.

Water he gets upstream of where the cattle drink;
his food he keeps fresh underground
lidded by slate, larder of berries and nuts;
sometimes, a trout palmed from the stream,
a rabbit caught by Ruff from the warren
in a moat where trees meet field.
He's watched him circle; delve; emerge,
limp body in his mouth, dog-proud.

Even in November, under storm clouds,
this is a good life, his most needs met,
memories. And he is an optimist.
His life is real. But yet he cannot still
his conscience. He cannot turn his back.
He knows the world beyond his wood
is broken: his song is sweet but frail
against the clashing dissonance beyond.

He wants truth not lies, ploughs not guns,
world fit for our daughters and our sons.

Towards Raven Wood

This evening I set out along the ridge across the valley, tracking my way to Raven Wood, following the route my adolescent steps once took.

Huge nests like thrown broomsticks, atop tall pines.....

In the wood below me, falling to the stream, my footsteps panicked a family of deer, their clatter echoing down the hollow.

The way was crossed by broken, bramble-ridden five-bar gates and barbed wire fences, a stream which forced a leap to mud and nettles.

Night swallowed evening, making each step on furrowed ground a hazard, only the moon, her face a handless clock, leaking light.

Huge nests like upside-down black, blown umbrellas, atop tall pines......

So I turned, not knowing if this scots pine copse still stood or had been razed by chainsaw, its place now levelled pasture.

The years pass. Raven Wood, between Upcott Barton and Down Farm, is dark-dyed through my fabric: ten or more tall pines,

and high in their canopies, at the uppermost, one hundred feet above the ground, huge nests, like tar-soaked driftwood palaces.

In age, I feel the urge to reach this wood; hope that these tall pine trees tower still, and over them still ragged ravens fly.

Holy Well

River and mill leat nourish this meadow
bound by roadway and granite bridge.
In the wood's lea, an older wall drops

to a Holy Well, built from stones cut
by hands so steady six hundred years'
doings have not prised them apart.

Monks found this Canaan in the woods,
husbanded cattle, nursed bees,
tended an apple orchard for their god.

The well mouth opens in an arch
over a slate-filled shaft, and each side
round baths brim with spring water.

This year, John Holland died here,
botched his hanging when the rope
broke, too weak to take his weight;

Evelyn Beer drowned here: too many
dank years cold in the Mill House,
under icy river water sunk her head.

Nose touching the cool wet, my tongue
tastes iron and thyme. I glimpse skeletons
of oak leaves on the water's bed

and my reflection shading the surface.

Wood Trout

Cleave, a field 500 feet above the sea:
flat as a cricket pitch to the west,
its south east corner drops
through a deep hollow to Towell Brook.

Its hedges are Devon style, turf on stone;
rabbits mine the brambled earth.
One post for the gate to the west
is a granite roller, one seasoned oak.

Ashes, oaks, hollies, honeysuckle
and a single service tree fringe Cleave
to the east; in this wood's shelter once
were fowl houses and three apple trees.

No towns black the map from Exmoor
to Dartmoor, Exeter to Bideford,
no sound but birds' caw and mew,
cattle low, chattering brook and church bells.

The grass is lush, grazed by bullocks,
dotted with rooks and red cartridges.
Locals, on humid autumn dawns, pick
mushrooms here, pearls in a green sea.

Through this field, where chicken scratched
the grass for corn, and men with hooks
and hazel switches trimmed the hedges,
a stranger to this ground I know,

I trace the footsteps of a dreamy boy
climbing Cleave, hazelnuts in his pocket,
a tiny tickled wood trout in his hand, lost
to the world beyond this field, and found.

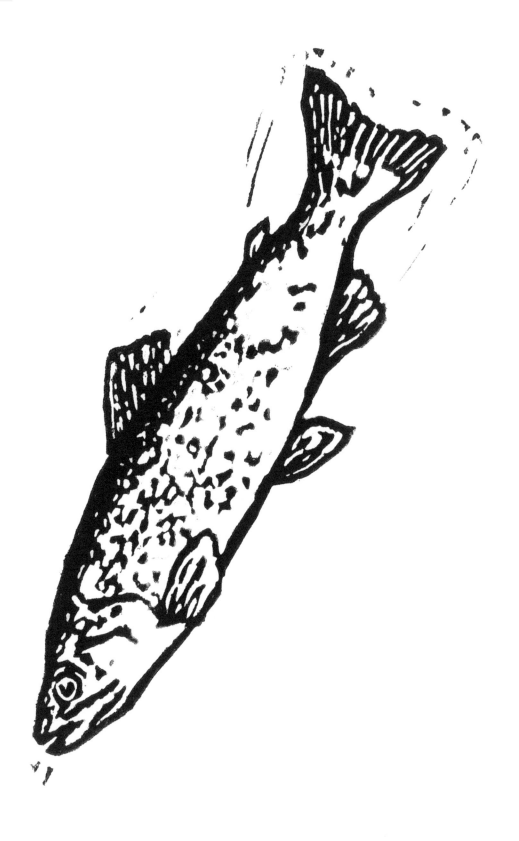

Tom in the Kitchen

See him bent to his Fergie, moon-grub,
nibbling light, nursing his machine on the field brow,
leaning to the slope, a giant silhouette ploughing
to the wood's edge. Twilight was no problem
to this man, whose drills
were straight as a homing crow's flight,
who left no idle ground. He finished
only when he'd done a proper job.
Not just a ploughman, this man
could thatch, dry stone wall, shear sheep
tick-tight, keep a garden like a kitchen table,
bake a cake air-light, and moist.

His wife and children did not stay
to see him calm his rage, his rumour-mongering;
never saw his loyalty, his need to give,
hear his weathered wisdom,
watch his flour-dusted fingers work a pastry
from dry and lardy flakes to crisp tart,
and, having fashioned a too-thin cigarette,
talk with love about those thunderous rows
between his prickly boss and him, and how,
from temper tantrums, weekend surliness,
and sudden, tender generosities,
there had grown a copper-bottomed trust.

Elizabeth Johnson's Path

You who've grown to know this land
paced it picnicked it
from Mill Lane through Hunters' Gate
past the weir up Strawberry Hill
and back around Harepath
tackled the anti-clock-wise walk
by day and under the night sky

or like the man visiting to fish
on a rented slice of river bank
hacked branches off
to sink his hook in Golden Pool
his diesel driven chainsaw din
stifling the slip of grit on slate,
find your feet have taken root
deep in this stuggy, sticky ground,

at your walk's high point
the Torridge snaking below
the gate to Halsdon Lane ahead
in bunched grass under the hedge
you'll spy an unobtrusive cast-iron plaque
these words inscribed:
'Elizabeth Johnson's Path, 1780'.

What urged this celebrated woman's solitary walk,
her treading and retreading the same track?
Was her mind mapping ocean voyages
far from these rolling, native hills?
Was walking how she calmed
and shaped her generative mind?
Did the stars, scattered like grain
over the Devon sky, nourish her piety?

Charlie Down, Labourer

His place was in his cottage window, latterly.
He'd sit there, darning hook in hand
fashioning doormats out of binder twine,
coils of patterned cord formed
oval mats for folk to use to clean
their boots of country mud and cowshit.
Through his glass he'd keep a tired eye
on The Globe Inn opposite, who entered,
left, after how long, who with and
in what state, who walked the main road
and why, or climbed Church Street
towards the graveyard and the church.

At dawn, young Charlie and his mate Perce
would leave their homes, cross the road
to Cooksworthy Lane, walk past the well,
beyond the fire pit and Rectory gardens
over the stone bridge spanning Towell Brook,
and up across two fields to Pearson,
where they'd snatch a necessary rest.
They were not built by brawn or inclination
to labour through the day, working all hours.
It was their routine rather to complete
their given task, lean on the nearest gate,
watch the seasons change and reminisce.

With binder twine they'd knot up sheaves,
fasten gates, braid cord to fashion ropes,
tie sheeps' legs, hang fowls from beams
then slit their throats. Though work to Charl
and Perce was labour, never offering
the gift of losing self in satisfaction,
they seldom missed a day at Pearson, put
luke warm hands to every task
allotted, and both men kept both hands,
unlike their neighbour Easterbrook whose verve
for trimming hedges led to one almighty swipe
and a one-armed handicap thereafter.

Between his years of labouring on the farm
and making mats, Charlie mended pushbikes,
in semi-darkness and the smell of three in one.
He fixed brakes and cables, chains and lamps,
but his first love was wheels, repairing
rear hubs, spokes and buckled frames.
With wrench and grease gun, ear
and eye, he worked on wheels, wheels
fixed to bikes, hung from the shed roof
or propped on his bench, bright as a field
of early morning spiders' webs, smiled
as a wheel spun freely with an oil-tuned hum.

Memorial Seat

She sits by the Torridge all day long
and all night,
a cotton frock made by her mother
covering her knees,

where they'd picnic, aunts, uncles,
children in frilly white dresses
eating wedges of pasty
round a cast iron kettle,
waistcoated men feeding the fire
and searching the ground
for flat pebbles to skim, hop,
hop, hop, over the river,

on an outcrop of sand and stone
among mares' tails,
rosebay willow herb, hazels,
and beached driftwood,
lifting their eyes at a splash
as a trout leapt
for mayflies, or a dipper
dove from a grey rock;

some nights a red deer will come to her
and she'll warm her hand on his back,
a moon silhouetting them
against the rushing water.

Her slate memorial seat settles
among oaks and wild garlic,
not for an age to be moved by
strong winds or by salt mists rotted.

Adam's Ale

For his last drink he cried for Beaford water.
Water: not a favourite wine or Irish whiskey!
Not beer brewed to an arcane recipe.
Beaford water! He wanted water from
an unassuming North Devon village
perched on a patch of scrubby heathland
between the River Torridge and Towell Brook.
This was his croaked and dying wish
to ease his chapped and bloodless lips.

Wine buffs, with a knowing sip, could name
with certainty the region, valley even
where the grapes were harvested.
A whisky drinker, too, could tell
as soon as dram touched tongue
whether he supped Laphroaig or Tomintoul,
know it by the flavour of its water.
If you drank water daily from your well
you'd know and grow to love its savour.

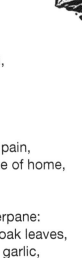

Grandfather, lying there, in nineteen fifties' pain,
pleading for Beaford water, craved the taste of home,
longed for his subtly tinctured liquid.
He could track the journey it had made:
from bed of Devon granite and clay counterpane:
through earth, a rich and native cheese of oak leaves,
bracken, trodden gorse, wild daffodils and garlic,
borage, grasses chewed by sheep and cattle,
to his pump: nightcap for a dying Beaford man.

Clovelly Cemetery

Small pebbles clack home like roulette balls,
Atlantic tides fidgetting
Gallantry Bower's rocky shore.

Sunshine, light clouds, a seagull floating,
a mowed meadow, Devon-hedged,
a cherry tree in May blossom by the gate.

Scattered in longer grass the gravestones list
in wavy rows, most slate,
some marble, one or two wood crosses.

Engravings of boats, steering wheels, anchors
grace some of the stones;
there are epitaphs to sailors.

One reads, after the dead man's name:
'Fisherman and Lifeboatman,
Home at Last, Safe in Harbour'.

If a passing stranger had to choose a place
to lay her head eternally,
here, on ancient rock, under white petals,
she would find a peaceful bed.

Lily Heard, born 1881

She died impatiently,
hungry for her son and God.

Left behind, her worldly goods,
none bequeathed:

a pestle and mortar, brass- because her cooking was so plain, its
    only use
perhaps was grinding herbs to complement her secret remedy for
    curing warts;

a desk, mahogany- smelling of acrid ink, and, in the drawers,
    assorted pens, nibs,
unassorted papers, paper clips, a photo album, monkey nuts, a
    desiccated orange;

her drop-leaf dining table: also mahogany, the other piece to catch
    the market's eye,
and, in its drawer, postcards from relatives, huge two-penny pieces
    and a horse brass;

her Singer treadle sewing machine: a family fantasy tells that Lil
    would of a night
hoist this much loved machine shoulder high and carry it over fields
    to dress-make
in Roborough (a walk of two long miles, over hills, a brook and stuggy
    marshland);

her thimble: it shines beside me on the window ledge, reminder of
    the times I'd thread
her needle; her hand stayed steady, though her eyesight weakened;
    but nothing
could stop her joining evening millinery class or making my wife's
    wedding dress;

her marital bed and feather mattress- she claimed with pride and
    paradox that she
had never once refused her husband; nor had he ever been allowed
    to see her bare;

her dressing table: made by her husband, a gentle carpenter who
    fashioned furniture
for village life: cradle, book case, window, table, rocking chair and
    coffin;

her kitchen clock: also in my room, a simple time piece but still
    ticking out time's toll
with a remorseless clunk, balanced by an optimistic chime that she'd
    hear every day.

That's about it, oh, and a chair or two,
some pictures, a ragged plant, a rug.

Her simple home was always open door
to maiden aunts, evacuees and passing souls.

If there's a heaven, she'll be there:
be with St. Michael at the gate

welcoming every breathless immigrant
with steaming cocoa and her home-made simnel cake.

In the Hall

And when the door to the hall
is shut they come.
Singly they come
or they come grouped in cloudlets like swirls of snow.

Why do they cluster together
at the stair's foot?
They stand mute
look cold as though aching for the warmth of touch.

She never fails to come,
my Grandmother
with her brother
holding her son's hand, lingering by the closed door

wearing the workaday
hat she herself
fashioned of mauve felt,
bedecked with plastic fruit set on a bed of tulle,

or in her Sunday best,
grey eyes steady
jutting chin whiskery
her broad back straight, mouthing Trust and Obey.

At the end, fatally sick,
and impatient to die
'Let me pass', she cried
glimpsing her long-dead son waving from the light.

I lie in my familiar bed,
remember those I've known
whose gravestones
now tilt, shadows dialing time on seeding grass.

I picture those gone:
instead of talk, silence,
instead of heat, absence,
hollow days, moments of ecstasy mere memory.

But their being
never fades.
By our sides
they walk, in our hearts they sing their translucent songs.

And when the door to the hall
is shut, they come.
Singly they come
or they come clustered like an impromptu, voiceless choir.

Joan 'n Arthur

The first names are 'Joan and Arthur.'
I delete 'and Arthur'
leaving 'Joan' alone
on this year's Christmas card list.

It won't be the last name I redact this year.
Down the page I add to last year's lines,
black through names and
through their hanging 'ands'.

The reaping has been done. Now with my pen,
like Time's apprentice,
I scythe the name out,
and another friend departs.

But what message do I send to solitary 'Joan'
when 'and Arthur'
indicates a coupling,
and after fifty years, a shared identity?

(The paradox is keen when 'and' shrinks to ''n',
as with Golding's Sam'nEric twins,
betokening a union so complete
that two souls bond to one).

For a half century they breathed
the same kitchen air, ate
at the same scrubbed table
where now she sits alone.

It's cool under the flinty Devonshire earth
on a hilltop among silver birch,
where Arthur's body
waits in his wicker cocoon:

above, the beat of horses' galloping
over the downs; at nightfall
the shuffle of badger and fox,
the fuss of tired birds settling.

I write some words of hope for Christmas
and the New Year, wanting
to address the card to Joan
'nFamily, Joan'nFriends.

And Arthur? Home in the ground,
his elements among tree roots
scattering over time:
Arthur'nMother Earth.

Why he stays

A shade fell from the chestnut tree,
over tilled soil from canopy to lawn
smelling moist of March-cut grass.
The falling sun nailed by the church spire
silhouettes rooks brawling in their churchyard
parliament, racketting among branches
careless of human cruelty and weather,
rooks, gloss-feathered gangsters,
mutinous sextons for the dead locked
tight beneath their granite gravestones.

But he's still here, beneath the chestnut tree he planted.
This motherless son of an absentee miner,
with not two pennies to rub together, married
the dressmaker's daughter, the joiner's daughter,
entranced by his dancing eyes over other eager lads,
built a family home, with hope and luck, retired,
and too soon, drained by a war wound, died.
No wonder he can't leave. He's here all right
(you don't even have to squint to see him)
leaning on his rake, skin brown as a nut,
fingers stained from Woodbines and Devon earth.

'Wakey! Wakey! Rise and shine! The time has come
the walrus said. You three are a pretty pair, if ever there was one.
Last night you stayed out till three o' clock this morning
and if you're going to stay here, you'd better clear out!'
words he used to wake us with each morning.
His wit is still the pulse of his once firm voice
now silvery, thinned by the pain of his last years.
Of course he can't leave. This is where he fought for.
When wounded on Montecasino's slopes
it was his wife and this soil pillowed his head.

Family Photograph

On whom do my eyes rest?
On her, who will be my mother,
though in this girlish moment, caught in a camera's click,
she's barely teenage.

Already she and her mother hold the stage,
her mother centre back (five family members either side)
cradling her bone china cup of tea,
a matriarch in black;

to grandmother's right, her son, cheekily smiling;
to her left, the daughter: limbs sturdy and long,
knees muddied from some tumbling escapade; both
oblivious to life's brevity.

This, their favorite picnic spot, is on the riverbank
against the now demolished weir, where,
among hazel saplings, stands
Mother's slate memorial seat.

She who will be my mother balances a plate of cake,
looks like west country yeastcake, in her lap,
leans back and smiles, her square jaw
sign of inner strength.

The Torridge flows towards the sea, and where the river
bends, the force of water over time has eaten out
the soft clay banks, undermined, uprooted
overhanging greenery.

This photograph, anonymously snapped between two wars,
portrays a world of innocent domesticity,
of unassuming country life,
of modest pleasures.

The pictured boy, carelessly smiling, dies of pneumonia
before the decade's done; his sister, growing up to be
my mother, so distressed, thereafter
cannot speak his name.

Two of the ageing maiden aunts marry older men, to happiness
of a kind. Then World War Two. My father volunteered,
returning with a gangrenous thigh-wound
and a shattered youth.

Had he not my mother for a wife, in this picture poised
like a spring seed, to nurse him through his agony
-a bedsheet's weight too heavy-
he would have died.

These two women, enduring as hard-seasoned oak, both
prizing optimism as their best possession, withstood
the world's worst. This brittle, fading photograph
celebrates their life.

River Gallery

1. Spring

This companionable river
buoyed my youth,
bore it on her too swift current,
might have encircled me,
but rushing to the sea,
looped early, found release
under Gallantry Bower,
the cliff on which her waters surfaced.

Flowing past she casts memories,
stripped, bleached trunks,
gnarled monuments
shaped by sun and rain; they collect
round Mother's slate memorial seat,
where the family picnicked-
where a weir
once slowed the river.

I dip my fingers
in the water,
begin to write.

2. Pigtails

Slices of parsley pasty
and Mother's egg custard tart,
make our tea,
appetites whet
by afternoon breezes
off shingle,
off broken oyster shells,
whet by our sprouting inches.

I tiptoe pebble to pebble
on the water's edge, step in,
hold cousin Althea's hand,
naked, skinny dipping
without knowing it.
Later, in bed,
we sleep,
her feet at my head.

A year on, picnicking there
with family friends,
I sit bewitched by Anne,
hair coiled in pigtails;
one runs down her back,
the other rings her chest.

3. Sundays

Past Shop Corner where the big boys nightly strut,
past Father's garaged car, eyes down,
scene of clammy trespass;
past the church, the village green,
Les Hooper's bull, steaming in his shed,
down Mill Lane, to the Torridge,
to Beaford Wood for daffodils,
single trumpetted natives,
they and wild garlic decking the banks
in pale yellow and white.
We brim our baskets, climb home,
to Spanish cream and chocolate cake,
to egg and cress sandwiches,
to Dena, perching on the sofa arm.
Once the grown ups leave the room,
she takes my hand, steers it
to her chest, squeezes.
Throat dry, I squeeze too,
fingers tingling, feeling
a never-before-felt spongy flesh.
I palm more ardently,
dare to pinch. She doesn't flinch.
Mother enters with the trifle.

Was it instinct, then, that led this barely teenage lad
up the stairs those Sunday evenings, creeping over
creaking floorboards to the bolted bathroom door,
where he'd steal to the keyhole,
watch his Mother, stepping naked from her bath,
towel her body down, dry first one leg
then the other, unconsciously
revealing to this suffocating boy,
as she turned and stooped,
twisted and stretched,
the flows, the dips,
the heavinesses,
the undiscovered contours of the female form?
Would this incestuous misdoing sap or warp me?
Could Mother see me bent behind the dimpled glass?
Was Sigmund watching in the shadows, taking note?

4. Sleep

Alone, except for isolated
shapes of jumbled body parts
hunched in desert sands
and paralysed. I'd wake
each Monday morning drained.

We rode our bikes towards a dump
for pram wheels, planning
posh trolleys,
down Mill Lane,
over Beaford Bridge,
and up the other side to Yeory.

At the brow of Mill Hill
my worn brakes failed.
I should have grazed
the hedge to slow me,
but clung on.

I sped, faster, faster, old lives flicking by:
Quarry Field where
I'd smoked bees from their beech tree home, for honey;
netted newts from their pond world, to die in jamjars;
held in my hand the beating heart of a shot hare.

My fate lay waiting
just before the bridge,
an aching corner, sweeping
left, steep, grit strewn,
sloping outwards.

I slewed across the road
hit hedge
flew
over handlebars
into hedge-top bushes.

Conscious,
and unhurt!
Hobbled home to Mother
dragging a buckled bike.
Put to bed
with tea and biscuits
to deep, untroubled sleep.

5. Sealed With A Loving Kiss

The weir is now slate shallows,
water combing weed-fringed rocks,
banks bristling with mares' tails and cow parsley.

Once currents swept away a wading sheepdog.
His workmate leapt to save him. Both dogs drowned.
This bony outcrop is our favoured picnic place.

Hair loose, Ann tugs her pullover.
We take her branches which she stacks
into a wigwam. She strikes a match.

I, twelve year elbows gawky,
watch her, as she, absorbed and fluid,
cooks batter, feeds the blazing fire.

The overweening letter I wrote later
-S.W.A.L.K. bold on the envelope-
was swooped on by the heron-eyed Headteacher.

6. Still watching

With the big boys to tall trees,
beech and oak, to high nests,
crow, magpie, hawk,
in the reek of woodbines
and the foxy armpit sweat
of men who'd worked all day.

He climbs. Hands shove his bum,
guide his feet to the first branch.
Face freckled, auburn hair
unkempt, he climbs
clinging to thin twigs,
inching to the kestrel's nest.

The trunk bends. He reaches up.
Fingers grope the nest.
Down he comes,
lands with a hop,
back to his mates
standing, waiting;

and, with flourish,
from his trouser pocket
withdraws a hand, brandishes
an egg, or, rather, fingers
wet with sticky yoke,
bits of jigsaw shell;

a pause, then, from his mouth
conjures a second egg,
whole and mottled,
the snub end brown,
his kestrel's egg.
I stand and watch.

7. Golden Pool

We reached Golden Pool, a stretch of deep
water, silent, expectant, amphitheatre
awaiting the main act; on one side a field
slipping to shingle, the other a crumbling

bank of sand, twelve feet high, honeycombed
with tunnels mined by martins hunting
insects in the milky sky above us, darting
in and out of nest-holes, feeding chicks.

Air was heavy, prickly with the scent
of thyme and dry thistle down. Shells
smelt of sea. Tarka swam these waters.
A brace of wild duck burst above our heads.

We lay on grass, face to face, marvelled how
the landscape drew round us like a fragrant
counterpane, then tiptoed off, leaving us
together, reflected in each other's eyes.

Her eyes were brown, wide, her body soft
as mine was hard, our breath interweaving,
our lips close. Our fingers blindly tracing
foreign languages, we talked through touch,

tenderly. In our careless youthfulness
we did not know that we would never be
as beautiful again, nor as content. We rose,
to face the old world in our newer skins.

8. To the sea

The river flows through Golden Pool
sifting sand, rattling her slates,
baring tree roots, easing earth away
as she homes toward Bideford Bay.

She's a cracked glass scarf trailed
between Devon hills, across pasture
and moorland, reflecting treasured
and forgotten images to passers-by;

a spool of film unravelled and coiled,
framing scenes that make the present
a gallery of epiphanies;
halting momentarily time's slip.

Past the ruined weir the river runs,
past Mother's slate memorial seat,
past Beaford Bridge off which
her second husband's ashes fell

like sleet towards their ocean bed.
Oblivious, the river tumbles on.
For those along her banks, she
leaves memories unsettling,

memories of hope: and, though
we cannot step into our same swift
flowing river twice, step in we must,
or we will merely stand and watch.

Milton Keynes UK
Ingram Content Group UK Ltd.
UKHW022331290224
438575UK00002B/24